POINT REYES

POEMS

ROBERT BLY

Point Reyes Poems

Robert Bly

MUDRA : HALF MOON BAY

1974

Distributed by Book People
2940 Seventh Street
Berkeley, CA. 94710

Cover illustration *Beach Rocks* from an
oil painting by Arthur Okamura
Photograph by Steve E. D'Accardo

Walking among Limantour Dunes

Thinking of a child soon to be born, I hunch down among friendly sand-grains . . . And the sand grains love us, for they love whatever lives with force not its own, a young girl looking out over her life, alone, without horses, with no map, a white dress on. . . . Whatever is not rushing blindly forward, the mole blinking at the door of his crumbly mole Vatican, the salmon sensing in his gills the Oregon waters crash down, or this planet abandoned here at the edge of the universe, the life floating inside the Pacific of the womb, near the walls, feeling the breakers roaring.

Sea water pouring back over stones

Waves rush up, pause, & drag pebbles back around stones . . . pebbles going out . . . it is a complicated sound, as of small sticks breaking, or kitchens heard from another house, good bodies turning over . . . then the wave comes down to the boulders, & draws out over the stones always wet, it is the gentleness of William Carlos Williams after his strokes . . . then the sound of harsh death waves racing up the roof of leopard stones, leaving a tiny rattling in the throat as they go out . . . and the ecstatic brown sand stretched out between stones, we know there are still young women who get angry.

And always another sound, a heavy underground roaring in my ears from the surf farther out, as if the earth were reverberating under the feet of one dancer, a comforting sound, like the note of Paradise carried to the Egyptian sands, and I hear the driftwood far out singing, and the great logs, fifty miles out, still floating in, the water under the waters singing, what has not yet come to the surface to float, years that are still down somewhere below the chest, the long trees that have floated all the way from the Pacific islands, and the donkey the disciples will find standing beside the white wall. . . .

November day at McClure's

Alone on the jagged rock at the south end of Mc-
Clure's Beach. The sky low. The sea grows more
and more private, the sky comes down closer, the
unobserved water rushes out to the horizons, horses
galloping in a mountain valley at night. The waves
smash up the rock, I find flags of seaweed high on
the worn top, forty feet up, thrown up overnight,
separated water still pooled there, like the black
ducks that fly desolate, forlorn and joyful over the
seething swells, who never "feel pity for themselves,"
and "do not lie awake weeping for their sins." In
their blood cells the vultures coast with furry necks
extended, watching over the desert for signs of life
to end. It is not our life we need to weep for. Inside
us there is some secret. We are following a narrow
ledge around a mountain, we are sailing on skeletal
eerie craft over the buoyant ocean.

Calm morning at Drake's Bay

A sort of roll develops out of the bay, & lays itself all down this long beach . . . the hiss of the water wall two inches high, coming in, steady as lions, or African grass fires. Two gulls with feet the color of a pumpkin walk together on the sand. A snipe settles down . . . three squawks . . . the gulls agree to chase it away. Then the wave goes out, the waters mingle so beautifully, it is the mingling after death, the silence, the sweep—so swift!—over darkening sand . . . the airplane sweeping low over the African field at night, lost, no tin cans burning, the old woman stomps around her house on a cane, no lamp lit yet. . . .

Trespassing on the Pierce Ranch

I walked toward Tomales Point over soaked and lonely hills — a wild cat runs away from his inspection of a wet gopher hole as I come near. Wind off the sea. A few sheep, cows with large udders high above the ocean. These are the first sloping lowlands the Eastern traveller saw as looking over the rail he suddenly came on a continent! In the middle of the endless ocean. And this is the frail land that thickens out into Nebraska, and the rocks that hold up the heavy pueblos.

Looking back east I see the three-quarters moon, moving in broad daylight, pale and urgent, through the sky. It moves slowly southward as the clouds flow past. It is an eye, an eye-traveller, going so alone . . . sturdy as an orphan. Bold and alone and formed long ago. Something compressed like us, compacted, then sent out again. It sails eerily forward just as we do. . . . I am separated from myself as it is from the earth . . . the two go along together. Half of me is down here . . . So I am what the ship's watch sees. Behind these lowlands the coast range, and behind that Nevada, and behind Nevada the running boys that the old men hit lightly with twigs, their heels hitting the earth drum, as they run toward the dancing ground, that has a stripped cottonwood tree at the center, and a sheep hanging high up on it.

Climbing up Mount Vision
with my little boy

We started up. All the way he held my hand. Sometimes he falls back to bend over a banana slug, then feels how lonely the slug is, and comes running back. He never complained, and we went straight up. What joy I feel in being with him! How much I love to feel his small leafy hand close around my finger. He holds on somehow, and we are flying through a cloud. On top we hunker down beneath some bushes to get out of the wind, while the girls go off to play, and he tells me the story of the little boy who wouldn't cut off his hair, and give it to a witch, and so she changed him into a hollow log! A boy and a girl came along, and stepped on the log, and the log said, "Ow!" They stepped on it again, and the log said, "Ow!" They stepped on it again, and the log said, "Ow!" Then they looked inside and saw a boy's jacket sticking out. A little boy was in there! "I can't come out, I've been changed into a hollow log!" (That's the end.)

Then I remembered a bit more: The boy and girl went to a wise man (he corrected me — wise woman) and said, "How can we get him changed back again into a little boy?" She said, "Here is a pearl. If a crow asks you for it, give it to him." So they went along. A crow came and said, "Can I have the buttons on your shirt?" The boy said, "Yes," and the crow took them all off. Then he saw the pearl on the shirt-pocket. "Can I have that too?" "Yes." Then the crow said, "Now we'll go to the witch's house." The crow started to drop some moss down her chimney. The chimney got full, the witch started to cough. He dropped in more moss. She had to open the door, ran outside! Then the crow took an oyster, a big one, from Johnson's Oyster Company, flew high into the sky and dropped it right on the witch's head. That was the end of her. And then the boy was changed back again into a little boy.

The land on top is bare, sweeping, forbidding. So unlike a little boy's mind. I asked him what he liked best about the whole walk. He said it was Bethany (an eight-year-old friend of Mary's) going peepee in her pants while hiding.

Finding a salamander on Inverness Ridge

Walking. Afternoon. The war still going on, I stoop down to pick up a salamander. He is halfway across the mossy forest path. He is dark brown, fantastically cold in my hand. This one is new to me — the upper part of his eyeball is light green . . . strange bullfrog eyes. The belly brilliant orange, color of airplane gasoline on fire, the back a heavy duty rubber black, with goose pimples from permanent cold. I make a kind of pulpit of my hand, and turn him upright; his head and front legs look out at me, the hands resting on my crossing thumb joint. In the warmth of the hand he grows more lively, and falls to earth, where he raises his chin defiantly. I pick him up again. But he is patient, this war, he can be held between a thumb and forefinger for many minutes, and the front paws hold on to your thumb resignedly—perhaps for hours. Perhaps it could be held quietly this way for days until it died, the green eyes still opening and closing. When I roll my hand over, I see the long orange-black tail hanging down into the cathedral of the open palm, circling back and forth, rolling and unrolling like a snake, or some rudder on an immensely long boat, a rudder that can't be seen by those on board, who walk up and down, looking over the hand-rail.

Sunday morning in Tomales Bay

For Michael and Barbara

The blue sky suddenly gone—fog all around—
we drift, lost . . . and north of us there's a machine
far away, a derrick . . . it is alive, it is a Great Blue
Heron! He turns his head and then walks away . . .
like some old Hittite empire, all the brutality for-
gotten, only the rare vases left, and the elegant
necks of their women . . .

Where he was, heavy bodies are floating—sea
lions! We float among them . . . the whiskered heads
peer over at us attentively, like angels called to look
at a baby . . . they have risen from their sea-man-
gers to peer at us. Their Magi come to them every
day . . . and they gaze at the godless in their wooden
boat . . .

After a while we drift nearer the fogged shore . . .
boulders on it in piles . . . sea-lions, hundreds of
them! Some on their backs playing, the whole shore
starts to roll seaward, barking and flapping . . . and
the heron slowly ascends, each wing as long as
Holland . . .

Now the lions have disappeared, they are some-
where in the water underneath us. At last one head
pops up five feet from the boat, looking neither ar-
rogant nor surprised, but like a billfold found in the
water, or a mountain that has been rained on for
three weeks . . . & the Great Blue Heron flies away
thin as a grassblade in the fog . . .

The dead seal near McClure's Beach

1.

Walking north toward the point, I come on a dead seal. From a few feet away, he looks like a brown log. The body is on its back, dead only a few hours. I stand and look at him. A quiver in the dead flesh. My God he is still alive. A shock goes through me, as if a wall of my room had fallen away.

His head is arched back, the small eyes closed, the whiskers sometimes rise and fall. He is dying. This is the oil. Here on its back is the oil that heats our houses so efficiently. Wind blows fine sand back toward the ocean. The flipper near me lies folded over the stomach, looking like an unfinished arm, lightly glazed with sand at the edges. The other flipper lies half underneath. The seal's skin looks like an old overcoat, scratched here and there . . . by sharp mussels maybe . . .

I reach out and touch him. Suddenly he rears up, turns over. He gives three cries, like those from Christmas toys. He lunges toward me. I am terrified and leap back, although I know there can be no teeth in that jaw. He starts flopping toward the sea. But he falls over, on his face. He does not want to go back to the sea. He looks up at the sky, and he looks like an old lady who has lost her hair.

He puts his chin back down on the sand, arranges his flippers, and waits for me to go. I go.

2.

Today I go back to say goodbye; he's dead now. But he's not—he's a quarter mile farther up the shore. Today he is thinner, squatting on his stomach, head out. The ribs show more—each vertebra on the back under the coat now visible, shiny. He breathes in and out.

He raises himself up, and tucks his flippers under, as if to keep them warm. A wave comes in, touches his nose. He turns and looks at me—the eyes slanted, the crown of his head like a leather jacket. He is taking a long time to die. The whiskers white as porcupine quills, the forehead slopes, goodbye brother, die in the sound of waves, forgive us if we have killed you, long live your race, your inner-tube race, so uncomfortable on land, so comfortable in the sea. Be comfortable in death then, where the sand will be out of your nostrils, and you can swim in long loops through the pure death, ducking under as assassinations break above you. You don't want to be touched by me. I climb the cliff and go home the other way.

The large starfish

It is low tide. Fog. I have climbed down the cliffs
from Pierce Ranch to the tide pools. Now the ec-
stasy of the low tide, kneeling down, alone. In six
inches of clear water I notice a purple starfish —
with nineteen arms! It is a delicate purple, the color
of old carbon paper, or an attic dress . . . at the
webs between fingers sometimes a more intense
sunset red glows through. The fingers are relaxed
. . . some curled up at the tips . . . with delicate rods
. . . apparently globes . . . on top of each, as at
World's Fairs, waving about. The starfish slowly
moves up the groin of the rock . . . then back down
. . . many of its arms rolled up now, lazily, like a
puppy on its back. One arm is especially active . . .
and curves up over its own body as if a dinosaur
were looking behind him.

How slowly and evenly it moves! The starfish is a
glacier, going sixty miles a year! It moves over the
pink rock, by means I cannot see . . . and into mar-
vellously floating delicate brown weeds. It is about
the size of the bottom of a pail. When I reach out to
it, it holds on firmly, and then slowly relaxes . . . I
suddenly take an arm and lift it. The underside is a
pale tan . . . gradually as I watch, thousands of tiny
tubes begin rising from all over underside . . . hun-
dreds in the mouth, hundreds along the nineteen

underarms . . . all looking . . . feeling . . . like a man looking for a woman . . . tiny heads blindly feeling for a rock and finding only air. A purple rim runs along the underside of every arm, with paler tubes. Probably its moving-feet. . . .

I put him back in . . . he unfolds—I had forgotten how purple he was—and slides down into his rock groin, the snail-like feelers waving as if nothing had happened, and nothing has.